BEAST

RELIEF

To know this truth of nature:
beyond the fleece of others
lie other beasts like you.

BEAST

Luke Morgan

ARLEN
HOUSE

BEAST

is published in 2022 by

ARLEN HOUSE
42 Grange Abbey Road
Baldoyle
Dublin D13 A0F3
Ireland
arlenhouse@gmail.com
arlenhouse.ie

978–1–85132–270–1, *paperback*

Distributed internationally by
SYRACUSE UNIVERSITY PRESS
621 Skytop Road, Suite 110
Syracuse
New York
13244–5290
supress@syr.edu
syracuseuniversitypress.syr.edu

Typesetting by Arlen House

cover image: 'The Púca' by Aidan Harte
is reproduced courtesy of the artist

CONTENTS

For my herd:
Mum, Dad & Jake

ACKNOWLEDGEMENTS

To the editors of the following journals and magazines: *Poetry Review, Poetry Ireland Review, Cyphers, Magma, Crannóg, Orbis, Skylight 47, Galway Advertiser, Banshee, Windows Publications.*

To Victoria Kennefick for the generous blurb. To Aidan Harte for the cover – I hope people talk as much about my poems as they do about your sculpture.

To my fellow Young Mystics – Maeve O'Reilly McKenna, Molly Twomey, Grace O'Doherty, Patrick Holloyway – for sharpening my snout. To my fellow Flinging Stys – Simon Costello, Georgia Way, Eoin Rogers, Ibrahim Hirsi, Susanna Galbraith, Suzanne Luppa, Roan Ellis-O'Neill, Ro Daniels and Louise Omer – for buffing my wings.

'An Irish Swan Remembers' was commissioned by Galway County Council to commemorate the centenary of the beginning of the Civil War in December 2021. My thanks to Josephine Vahey for picking me as one of her horses. 'The People of Moynoch Hills' was the winner of Windows Publications' 19th National Student Poetry Award in 2012.

To the mentors: Ciarán O'Driscoll; James O'Toole, Vox Galvia; Nidhi Zak/Aria Eipe; Damian Gorman; Jessica Traynor for helping hands. To all at Poetry Ireland – Liz Kelly, Jane O'Hanlon, Moira Cardiff, Anna Bonner, Paul Lenehan, Colette Bryce – for continued support. To Louise Ryan and Nóirín Ní Fhlathartha. To the pupils of Merlin College, Galway – for showing me what poetry should be, and how it absolutely shouldn't.

To my friends and family who recorded some early versions of these poems in their own voices – my darling Jenn Pond, Jake Morgan, Claire Ahearne, Kenny Gaughan, Seosamh Duffy, Suzie Ryan, Lelia Doolan, Nadia Ramoutar, Frances Jones, Nithy Kasa, Yvette Picque, Katie O'Connor, Jackie Davy, Jackie Roantree, Jo Webb, Anna and Gus O'Donnell, Rebecca Stiffe, Magda Konczyk, Fintan Geraghty, Stephanie Brennan, Eileen and Niall Humphreys, Daniel Mulcahy, Maria Morgan, Bernie Duffy, David Curran, Eddie Connolly, Ciara Wall, Anne Curran, John and Christine Valters Paintner, Audrey Gidman, Deirdre Curran, Robert Morgan, Iva Grillo Gannon, Ita Reddington, Jim Curran, Deana Nic Uidhir, Luke Palmer, Jarlath Tivnan, Sarah O'Toole and Colette Devaney.

BEAST

A Brief History of Hair

'Hair plays a key role in the defence mechanisms of most fur-bearing animals.'

– *Bernstein Medical Journal*

Once upon a time, I climbed an iron gate
and got my forehead licked by a heifer.
Most of the saliva came out in the shower,
but there remained a cowl above my eyebrow;
timid at events I'd allow
relatives to praise what I did not create.

Soon my quiff was lost beneath some quills
I stole from porcupines in the garden
which started stabbing me to harden
my scalp against a bully's insults.
Yet, behind the courts, a girl once raised my pulse
by stroking them aside until they stilled.

Next, I had a peacock block my lonely climb
before the Hill of Doon, so I offered
follicles of hair. In return he prospered,
made his dazzling nest in my trousers.
On the internet, in one too many browsers,
I gazed at others, not content with mine.

Dad came to my rescue when the time was near
and strands began to fade from my thin crown.
Naked mole rats scared me, vultures stared me down,
but I realised what was needed;
lifting honest shears, advice at long last heeded,
I shaved away my guises without fear.

Self-Portrait as Mandrake

Was it me who was pulled into the world
purple, clumped umbilical and strangled limb,
hung upside down and smacked, shrieking?

Or was I the yellow child,
kept in a glass box
until blood filled the tips of my ears?

The soil echoed our breaths
as we bent into it,
black smears across our brows,
whipping tendrils into a wheelbarrow.

I watched our dad,
the veins from the soft insides of his elbows
reaching to the backs of two muddy hands.

I thanked heavens for the rain.
When he'd call, I'd feel phone lines tighten
constricting the mountains in Connemara.
Instead, the only sound

was our reaching
into the wet ground we'd come from,
the gasping as we tore it open
again and again.

Beware the Bull

We had one behind our house
though I never saw it,
not once.
Its smoky anger was made real by whispers –
estate kids claiming they saw O'Malley
lead a giant black cloud on a leash
into the field at night
where it waited, daring us
to get close enough to run away.

In my head it looked like the one
my dad had drawn on our kitchen wall –
form lost in smudges of charcoal,
horns a panic of white
on brown parchment.
The more I studied it
the less sure I grew of its outline,
moving in and out
of hazy nightmare.

Its maker moved around the house
while I lay in bed. I knew him
by the creak of the top stair,
bursts of air through his nostrils.
When he left, so did the picture.
I never asked whether it was real or not,
whether the adults just kept us in fear
to stop us straying away
from the tidy safe pens of our homes.

KELPIE

My sister was born a kelpie
on the wrong side of a frozen lake.
Our dad never spoke about it,
but one Christmas, he took
my brother and I out to Connemara
to find her ashes
in a camper van with no brakes.
The place was coated in stillness,
the road granite spangled under white.
We stopped at every beat
of water we came across,
retracing steps, asking
if this was the one that held
our mythological sibling.
At Lough Inagh, my breath cast
embryonic statues
that evaporated in mid-air.
This wasn't the place, he said,
but through the clouded glass
I thought I saw
the glowing eyes of a horse,
mildewed reins around her neck
like umbilical cords shaping out
endless question marks
in the deep.
Dad told us they'd deliberately picked
somewhere unknown, hard to reach,
and after our toes turned
numb, we gave up.
On the way home,
there was a crossroads
with a car approaching on the right.

Dad pulled the brakes
before he remembered they were gone,
and while the other car beeped,
I watched him simply take his hands
off the wheel,
as our great tainted vessel
was carried through the junction
on a sea of fabled ice.

THE HYDRA

Though he won the battle, he lost the war.
When I told him of the four boys at school
he ignored the principal, burst their door
like a Hercules seeking Hydra drool.

When I told him of the four boys at school,
he at last admitted this was his quest
like a Hercules seeking Hydra drool
but he found this monster had many heads.

He at last admitted this was his quest
with his son embittered and clearly shook,
but he found this monster had many heads
which the necks regrew every time he struck.

With his son embittered and clearly shook,
he did slice and quarter, did maim and slay,
but the necks regrew every time he struck
unaware meanwhile if I was ok.

He did slice and quarter, did maim and slay,
he ignored the principle, burst their door
unaware meanwhile if I was ok,
though he won the battle, he lost the war.

GODMOTHER

First thing I remember
is the pond in Nutley Lane
she saved me from.
Lilies and willow pollen
formed a skin that bobbed
when I touched it,
and suddenly, I was underneath
in a murky bloodstream,
frantic rosary bead bubbles
carrying the last of my air
upward.
I could have stayed there forever,
until she appeared,
more beautiful than I'd ever imagined,
a fish tail petrol-shiny and flapping
between us. She held me
as we spiralled up,
spun in the tangle
of her weightless hair,
tasting sky then in wide,
hungry gulps.

The next time I saw her,
she wore her skin over dry bones.
I've searched for her tail
in every photo since,
every absent memory,
but now, above water,
I finally see the black
of her eyes,
her hair cut short,
how we've both grown legs.

EIGHT ARMS

When I was born,
my parents told me
I had eight arms.

They also said
my blood was blue
and if I cut

one arm from me,
it would grow back
longer, stronger.

A miracle
I learned to walk
with those suckers.

I often wish
a skeleton
would keep me still

while I'm sleeping,
a single brain
could be relaxed,

and in my chest
there was one heart,
not three.

Though long ago,
all mirrors show
I believe them

still.

OCTOPUS

Mum mopped the floors with an octopus.
I'd watch between the bannisters,
warned to stay upstairs
until she'd spread its slime
through the house.

The tentacles slapped and sucked,
a writhing gorgon head
she'd cut from the shoulders of a beast.
Jaw clenched, top lip swallowed,
she lathered it all on the floor:

dad's reaction to the lock change;
her new department head who'd pushed
a sweaty 50 note into her palm –
clouds of inky smoke
rising behind her as she moved.

When I'd walk the ground again
I'd realise it was still damp,
that my footprints
on the black tiles
were shaped like tiny fan-tailed squid.

ONE IN A COLONY

I led us through the subway –
12, the only one who knew
where we were going.
But once I saw her on the other side
of the closing doors
and the platform slid out of view
like a polar ice cap falling
into a pitch-black ocean,
Manhattan suddenly became
an Antarctic colony
of suited-and-briefcased emperors
towering over me, beside me,
in front of me, behind me,
stinking of rotting fish
the blubber of their faces
hiding cold eyes that I sought out.

Later, she told me
how a penguin can pick out
their young in massive crowds.
How she got on the next train
and waddled out at each station
scanning through endless streams
of black and white.
But I didn't know any of that then
hurtling beak-first through darkness
with no phone, no hotel address,
no money, no overhead intercom to page.

At our destined stop, I sat
and breathed statues into the air
while the ground melted around me.
How many million penguins
I don't know for sure

but when she stepped out onto the rink
and put a fin to my panic
I saw them all through her eyes
and noticed my own mouth
standing out like a flame
among the monochrome crowd.

THE STARFISH

Three months after they left
there was a smell in the bedroom of death.
Fourteen and Twelve, they had no luggage
when we collected them
standing on the muddy tiles of Galway train station
except for brown paper bags worn thin
with the ghosts of apples.

Penneys did the trick. One of our hoodies fitted,
though it was tight.
They had square-framed glasses,
spoke a language full of throat,
flashed wide teeth in frequent smiles.
The Chernobyl boys. So good
at football, in estate games,
you couldn't have them on the same team.

Once they had gone home
the smell began to haunt the hall
like an invisible enemy.
We finally discovered tucked between a mattress
and the wooden panel
a starfish, pulp as bruised fruit,
soaked with the sweat of its own decaying,
the scaly skin unnatural and cold.

We wrapped it inside a bag inside a bag
and wheeled the bin from our house.
We washed the gunk from our hands
while our eyes watered,
the memory already shrivelling
a slow and permanent fade
until all I see now are the square-framed glasses,
those wide and terrifying teeth.

ALTITUDE SICKNESS

Did you know that a change in altitude
can make you shit yourself?
I didn't. Standing, old enough to be mortified,
in the cubicle of a Pyrenees resort,
while Jake disappeared down the Red Slope
by himself. One of the instructors
(his name was Jesús) sounded the alarm
and off sliced a search party of adult knives,
penduluming the half-pipe of ice.
I hadn't gone beyond Baby Blue
but I recall that whirling descent
as though I was there,
hurtling arse-first through annals
of my own turboed bloodstream.
This is how it happens, I panicked,
swinging over and back between
newspaper headlines
and the apple yoghurt goatee
of my never-to-be-found brother.

It turned out he was sitting off-piste
unaware of the fuss he'd caused. By dinner,
we had learned to laugh about it.
I learned that day what it meant
to be struck by the dizziness
of height, to be shocked by my own stench,
to be left helpless to the inward slopes
I once thought I could control.

ZAMBIA

Nobody move. Boyd, our driver,
hand daring towards the rifle on his belt.
No windows. Hardly a roof.
We were dead.
She placed so deftly alongside us
it was as though the sky was on a conveyor
and she, perfectly still.
She stared at me. Everything
got swimmy –

like when we were kids
and Jake threw a rock at the back
of my head.
Look. I showed him my crimson hand,
in stupid awe of its stickiness
between my fingers, its persistence
in every tiny tract of my skin,
and he, face crumpling,
certain he had killed me,
running to the end of the garden
to await his lifelong punishment
of silence.

The lioness opened her mouth
and licked that blood from my fingers.
Her tongue was warm
as a nurse's voice.
Then, almost bored, she turned back
to her cubs.
I touched her saliva to the back of my head
where the hair has stopped growing
and remembered the soft instruction –
Sleep on your side for a few days, don't scratch,
and try not to get caught out in the rain.

CONGER

And then there was the day
I nearly lost you your tongue.
Remember? On the Palmers' trampoline
creeping up while you were mid-somer
-sault. Thrown, you landed
on the crown of your head,
your teeth making gumdrop rubber
of the conger eel in your mouth.

It held itself by a thread
against the flow and ebb of blood.
I could barely look
and you could barely wail
but years later, in a place faraway from me
it emerged again from its coral,
introducing itself
at conducting workshops,
flapping at basement comedy gigs,
wrapping around awards speeches
to rooms full of crisp reef flowers.

Until you came back here,
and were out-congered to a stony cave.
This time, I didn't mean
to sneak up on you,
I didn't mean to shut your teeth
on your glistening, dancing voice.

RODENT

I woke to feel his nimble claws inside me
and scratched away the thoughts of my own death.
My aunt Joann – the first resort next door –
pressed a hand against my wheeling chest
to find a frightened creature racing there.

Next day, I felt a nurse spread cold blue gel
and for the first time in my early life,
could curse my misbehaving pet on screen.
'We'll need to make a cut right here,' she said,
'but not before you're twenty nine years old.'

I nailed some wood against my ribcage then
and sought the noise to hide me from his squeaks.
When that backfired, I tried to pawn him off –
showed him to some strangers after dark
who turned him upside-down until he squealed.

The day I lay my head upon your chest,
I heard a scuttle faint and turned to look –
a grey-haired thing stared back with beady eyes;
this once-forgotten pest, despite my best,
had run me here with all his furry might.

THE LAST OF THE RHINOS

While the final rhinos are being sniped
I'm learning about my body through porn.
The glow of the laptop a cold sun,
another humongous body turned by forklift.

Teachers, nature documentary presenters,
my dad stopping by a ditch
en route home from the zoo to have a piss,
I beg them to turn around and reassure me.

Google says 5.1 inches
so, I aim steel rulers against me
careful not to hit a vein and bleed out
over my grey uniform.

I want to close tabs
where pleasure-wrinkled foreheads
look like heat-dried hide
but the question is how to look on
as the next beast falls,
and in the poached silence, tell myself
I'm not yet the last of my species.

ARMADILLO

Here's how he'll arrive:
not with a thud
but a nuzzle,
so slight you'll barely notice him.
In Mrs Divilly's geography class
learning about rock formations
no less. You'll never
wear loose boxers again.
Hiding from a hall roll
of loud students
in the furthest cubicle, the one
with a thick stone wall on one side,
he will unfurl
in your terrified hands,
look up at you,
beg to be protected.
Curl back into a ball then,
still too visible
behind your trousers.
'Alright there, Lukey?' Lads
will stop your heart at the lockers,
smile knowingly when you claim
it's just a seam in the fabric.

Listen for him that first night,
make a locked room ambient,
breathe onto palms to try and coax him,
but know he is unpredictable
and will emerge
at the most confusing of times –
stupid o'clock on a freezing bus,
mid-quadratic equation after lunch,
in a changing room full of bony classmates.

You will lose him
on a day in January
when a girl with tamed fire for hair
walks to you across the green of your estate.
Don't panic. Play some
Stevie Wonder on the old hi-fi
in the living room.
Let him go to her.
Feel his gentle weight leave your body
and don't for a second be sad
that he does not look back.

PITCH

Before everything got complicated,
there was the Rugby Schools' Cup Final.
I stood on a pitch
more bullet hole mud than grass
and held out my hands.
Richter Scale Rogers
plucked it from the ruck
and ran it himself
before hitting the ground.
Comerford, carrot-top hair,
freckles in the shape of a smile
retrieved it and flung it at me,
a yell let sail through gleaming gumshield.

Within a year, Rogers and Comerford
were gone, a shock
passed from one to the other,
before nestling against my chest.
The rest of us are still here,
our legs pumping
against defensive lines,
madmen in the sludge
trying to stay on our feet.

THE FRONT PAGE

when everything crashed
and the government bailed out the bondholders
my dad and brother dressed up as tuxedoed pigs
and stood outside the department of finance
dancing and throwing fake money at everyone

their skin was painted luminous pink
their stereo blaring
the sight of them toasting glass chutes of apple juice
paused the morning commute on merrion street
for several minutes

they got on the six-one news that evening
and when the school secretary rang home
the next day to ask why he was absent
my mum replied
look at the front page of the *independent*

there they were
cardboard snouts so lifelike
the bright facepaint
like someone had taken a highlighter pen
to all that black and grey

The Search for the Mastodon

1806, USA: It's rumoured the real reason behind the Lewis and Clark Westward Expansion is to find the Mastodon.

Jefferson re-arranged her bones
nightly on the floor of his study
until he had a skeleton he could believe was real.
Obsessed she still roamed the land
like a dream caught in an empty hall,
he ordered the doomed quest
two centuries before I sat on a plane
destined for an unknown west
imagining the horns that waited for me.

A campfire circle heard of my ten-foot-tall beast
though I hadn't yet been the one to find her.
Leathered skin, tame enough for a leash,
oblivious she could crush me in a heartbeat.
I excavated the soil beneath a circus tent
using tusks given me by another traveller
but the sunken skull we found
belonged to a mere elephant
and we went again our separate ways.

Lewis and Clark returned empty-handed.
I scoured the streets
of the greatest city on Earth;
breaching chain-link around vacant lots,
siphoning through wall ornaments
in neon dive bars after dark,
hearing brays from her trunk
in the scrape of alleyway dumpsters,
foreign wheels on flooded tar.

When I returned at Terminal Two,
a crowd clambered against the rail
to hear of the failed crusade.
My eyes went above the searchers
to one so huge she filled the room –
these bones I knew from a study floor,
these teeth I'd shut in a glass corner case,
together now as something more,
a myth come true inside a face.

ELEPHANT

You handed me an elephant.
Plush, straight-lined, soft to rub.

I didn't know what to do with it,
this tiny perfect thing.
It sat above the spare mattress in my room
and everyone I knew rejoiced at it.

But I already had an elephant. This one
was large and ugly. It filled each room
and stomped to announce itself
at the worst
of times. Up close it
smelled of piss and sweat and I
thought I would choke
if it
sighed at
me.

I was more afraid of yours.
It called out to be held, looked at me
with glass eyes,
took on the smell of wherever it slept.

So, I gave it away.
It was a poor trade for you, anyways.
You handed me an elephant
and all I handed you
was a fox.

SCAVENGER

Only the furry orange of a streetlight
through the curtains
when I heard the rustling
in the stillness of a satellite town.

The bin was overturned.
It picked through plastic packaging,
old apple cores, the stir-fry
we couldn't finish.

I didn't call out. I just stood,
not sure I wasn't dreaming,
afraid to breathe in case
it looked at me

and I saw, through mirrored eyes,
a lonely creature,
in search of anything
that might give it peace.

TOUGH STUFF

I can't go beat the shit out of him
and I certainly can't go beat the shit out of her
so I decide to go beat the shit out of the Atlantic
instead.
'Come on so' it shouts at me,
thumping its chest
but, as we all know,
the worst kind of person to taunt
is the person who is prepared to die
and I am
I'm bloody well prepared to die
so I kick off my shoes trousers socks jocks
and run into it
and it thumps me
but I thump it back
it grabs my balls and puts me
into a headlock and pulls my hair
until we're both out of breath
and we walk to the shore together
our arms around one another
and it says to me,
'You're made of tough stuff, man –
you're made of tough stuff.'

VILLANELLE OF THE PÚCA

To many people once, I could be many things
and seeing me would only bring bad luck;
but I found my shape in all the shape-shifting.

With many lovers once, I did have many flings –
I rode until the ground beneath me shook;
to many people once, I could be many things.

For undeserving hearts, I chose the word that clings,
the word that leaves its searcher rare and struck;
I found my shape in all the shape-shifting.

I am ashamed to say I clipped a fair few wings
and more to say I kept the ones I took;
to many people once, I could be many things.

I thought I sat at tables meant for worldly kings,
grew a brittle fur you couldn't pluck;
I found my shape in all the shape-shifting.

Now the fattened lady chortles as she sings,
you will no longer see me run amok –
to many people once, I could be many things,
but I found my shape in all the shape-shifting.

MOBY

I felt it before I saw it – a deep rumble
and then, so large it took a minute to realise
I was looking at a single eye
and not a solar eclipse,
the water cascading down its dark leathery skin,
it swallowed the entire ferry
and everything went black.

I woke on a flap of wood
floating in a small lake
vaulted with flesh walls,
a drip from somewhere near
knelling down the seconds like a horrible clock.
There was to my eye not a single survivor but me.

I passed the time by walking,
the squelch of my feet on the moveable ground
a sound I knew were I ever to escape
I would never forget.
I watched the innards contract and release,
spit hectolitres of mucus-tinged water
and tried not to get my hair wet.
I ate the fish I found flapping loosely in small puddles,
cut them with a penknife I saved
from a windbreaker jacket in the lake.
I eventually got used to the sudden lurches,
loud as creaking skyscrapers,
and taught myself to sleep again
using a form of mind meditation
I always thought to be useless.

And then, just when I had resigned myself
to be happy with the life I had already lived,
I was freed.

There was a bubbling on the surface
and before I could stand, my wood and I
were blasted upwards –
my exit through the blubbered cap-ring
like a second birth.
I gasped my way to shore,
sitting on the sand
while its awesome tail smacked the sea again
creating waves that reached my feet,
broke apart and returned, defeated, to the deep.

Of course, nobody believed my story.
What does it matter? I avoid
fish at all costs now,
and will not step on a boat.
Sometimes, in the belly of night,
I hear a deep groan
that undercuts my petty worries
and see the huge eye again
like a black sun
holding back a terrible, brilliant light.

TAPEWORM

Dad told me when I was younger
that the way to nab a tapeworm
was to dangle a Mars Bar in front of your arse,
and when it peaked its nose out,
grab it and keep pulling
as though you were unravelling a shoelace knot.
This, while he crushed a white tablet to powder
and mixed it with jelly
so that Sparky wouldn't suspect a thing.

I went to a witch doctor in Shrule.
She made me hold a steel handle
that was hooked up to a strange machine
and told me I had a tapeworm.
6 foot long, she said, pointing it out
on the screen, a series of coloured squares
highlighting something that looked
no more like a worm
than an ultrasound looks like a child.

It did make sense. For years,
I'd been having stomach problems –
our GP diagnosed IBS, and I went through
phases of spelt bread sandwiches
in my lunchbox, which had the sharp aftertaste
of wine mum let me try once.
When that didn't work, I returned
to the honesty of white loaves,
resigned to my lifetime of cramps.

The doctor was from South Africa
and as she took me through my body maths,
she shared some incredible stories.

Among her claims to fame was Brad Pitt's six-pack;
she'd worked with him as a dietician
when he was doing *Fight Club*. Dad showed us
that film when we were too young,
and to this day, when I think of sex scenes,
I see Helena Bonham Carter's cake-icing belly.

Apparently, the thieves in Cape Town
will come during the day to slit open your dogs
so they will bleed out by nighttime and won't bark.
Bengi has fourteen stitches and I put every one
of them in myself. I stared at her huge dog
who'd greeted me when I arrived,
pictured his pale pink guts on the pavement
and her pushing them back in, gently
zipping him up tight.

The pharmacy sold me pills
and I took one every day for two weeks.
I peered into the toilet constantly,
expecting to see my tenant, taller than me,
piled up like a horrible brain in the loo water.
When I didn't, I briefly considered
the Mars Bar.

Turns out it was onions.
I trusted a FODMAP chart
and the pains vanished overnight.
I Googled the parasite then
and found a picture in a medical journal,
circular fangs encasing its big mouth
like something out of a half-remembered film,
wondered how on Earth I'd ever believed
a single word they told me.

STAG

The lads were all born-again Christians.
We stayed up late around a fire
slugging Karpackie and flicking blunts.
The funny accents soon turned
to whooping from my sleepless nights –
I found myself cheering
to the foreskin of a cackling man.
Another one took a clicking lighter's tongue
to his patchy pubic hair.
We ended things in peals of sick,
then off they went with praying hands.

I heard the quips I'd heard before
in passing herds of lower men;
how we'd vow to press a girl's
cheek against a bedroom wall.
My sodden camping gear
sweating through black plastic bags,
I drove on through the Wicklow rain
until a flash of jumping fur
stopped my car with a screech,
leaving me a ghost imprint
of fragile hide, of two big glaring horns.

Diary of a Pangolin

'following the killing of two pangolins, sexual intercourse in the village was banned.' – *stolen from an academic report*

And what's more, diary,
they stopped speaking to each other.
Huts curled up into keratin domes,
nails that used to trace veins
on sweating backs
were now hiding in their owners' mouths,
bitten off and falling
to the ground like dry petals.

We were dead, diary,
but even we could detect
the stiffness;
the woman returning from the market
with bulbous zucchini,
her husband with his nose
close to cheese that smelled like her.

We were dead, diary, our bodies hung
from the tribesman's door
like dressing robes that long for bath hour.
But only we could hear the two youngsters
tiptoeing into trees at night,
the whisper of their skin against bark,
the gasp of busy hands
as they climbed inside the shell of one another
and came up for air.

THE PROMISE

I go back to the moment
I was nearly never born.
1931 and my great-grandfather
is driving a truck in a hardware yard
in Clones, Co. Monaghan
when he runs over a child.
The mother puts a curse on him
and over the next two years,
his wife kneels on cold tiles
and counts three miscarriages
in the loo basin. As she weeps
into net curtains,
he resigns himself to
the echo chamber of the dawn walk –
a pendulum of baby cries
on his way to work,
the sun behind the horizon
damp brown.

Further. Ancient times.
The Nile has flooded.
Spokes of floating wood
leave dimples in the mud water.
Women pray for days, but the hippos
wander through their carnage anyway,
taking babies out of straw baskets
and chewing them alive.
Men flee. Driven dizzy,
one town sacrifices a little boy
on a makeshift altar that sinks
in heavy sand. Within a week,
the river finally contracts
like a settled womb.

My great-grandmother is not praying
to the God she thinks she is.
Taweret with the swollen belly sits
by her side each night, listening
to all the lives the woman
has to bargain with.
I am only a grain of sand
three grains deep,
but I look this hippo in the eyes
and plead for my life.
It seems to be enough. Inside nine months,
Taweret has given her stomach
to my great-grandparents
and the boy that arrives
has my eyes, has the mouth
I used to make my sacred promise.

* Taweret, the ancient Egyptian goddess of childbirth and fertility,
takes the form of a hippo.

SAVAGES

Terrible things happened.
Nanook and his fellow sailors, days without food,
dragged the huskie in from its perch
and stoned its head for furs.

Or the sludge-backed walrus, caught lagging
when the horde up-and-hurried for waters,
reeled in by spear rope – 'the Tiger of the North'

weighing limp in the burnt-white surf
as Nanook licked blood off a blade
as long as her tusks.

And years spent crafting the snow
into polar bear shapes
for target practice, to work the arrows –
Nyla his mate chewing sealskin
to keep stiffness from the leather,
stabbed earlier through the geyser hole
when it came up for air.

But when the voice of fellow man
canned within the gramophone
hits Nanook's ears,
the Eskimos lean closer,
fall around the floor in awe and laughter,
and later dream of *why*,
touch noses with noses.

THE PEOPLE OF MOYNOCH HILLS

Days the weather cleared for them;
an annual cattle market, a familiar
assemble at the St Patrick's parade.

Only knowing faith as Sunday mornings,
gold port after funerals.
Hooded youths would marry into a family
their own family knew

and stopping over to visit one of the old churches,
you'd see heads almost scratching themselves –
whispers to equals beside them, known since birth,

but you had no idea of glass shards
in derelict houses – that down nameless,
pretty lanes after closing time in the bars,
strangers were not welcome.

SMALL ORANGE SUNS

Where I'm from, they used to turn
the streetlights off at night
so the birds wouldn't think it was daytime.
The constant chirping through the small hours
fooled us – once, I got out of bed
and dressed at 4am.
The night became the night then,
the only brightness from sweeping headlights
of lone cars, the truncheons of trains.

In the morning her body was found,
slit in private places, hair matted
with dirt. Two men were questioned
and let go. Those living in houses nearby
saw nothing, but some recalled
a small, stifled cry –
imagined or real, they couldn't tell –
one as delicate as a wren would make
under the small orange suns.

IN THEIR OWN PACKS

I once heard Ms Yew watched her husband
mauled by wolves
on the other side of a wire fence,
and as I sit outside her grocer
licking icing from my thumbs,
I try not to think about
her standing there, screaming,
while muffled snarls rip him apart
and carry him into darkened woods.

When she first arrived –
so tall she set the women talking –
we invited her son up to the estate
and she sashayed him up the tarmac
like sweetness in the frost.
My friends and I agreed poor Kristof
was no playmate – 'a funny smell off him' –
and mothers hushed us inside
when she'd pass again, lashing on

the glaze of names.
A woman like Ms Yew, everyone reasoned,
was not to be trusted.
She'd be just as well
taking that smelly son of hers
back to where she came from –
where pastries are not delicacies,
where animals in the night
roam in their own packs.

An Irish Swan Remembers
after 'The Children of Lir'

Running from a flaming Post Office
and shoving the barrel of a rifle
down my brother's neck.
December 1921 and, until today,
it was the last time I spoke to him.
He'd opened his mouth to plead
before I'd heard the voice of our father
screaming a spell we knew
from an old storybook
and next thing we were away out
on the laps of Lough Corrib
flapping murderous wings at one another
while men on the shore
buried their noisy dead.

One hundred years I spent
visiting each shingled island
trying to find another way to spite him.
Every swan I fell in love with
withered and sank eventually
like heavy linen in the murk water.

Until I met my brother again
at The Claddagh in Galway,
our feet still webbed, feathers dripping,
ignored by the child
with the tri-coloured loop-de-loop,
by the juggler who tossed shapes
that looked like countries.
We didn't recognise the tongues we heard.
And so, we looked at one another
laughed at our cursed immortality

until we grew fingers again
and felt our skin crease with the creak of years.
Holding ourselves against the cold,
our eyes went to the canal
where a swan drifted straight and proud
as the white between two flags.

WHAT ROMULUS SAW

'Rome wasn't built in a day'
but our mum watched us destroy it in one.
Forget crumbling marble,
iron daggers sunk in turned backs.
I'm talking about the very beginning,
the two of us on the banks of the Tiber,
naked in the sand.
She approached us as a wolf,
disbelieving our rare pink.
But it was us who would eat her,
put her nipples into our mouths,
feel cities return to our cheeks.
My brother died that day.
I pushed him further down her belly
and she gazed at me
between fear and pride,
ready for the grip around her neck.
I drank my fill, saw the pantheons
we'd build in her eyes,
and when they caught the light
I saw the whole place set ablaze.

SELF-PORTRAIT AS TROJAN HORSE

I'm tired of whinging.
Just wheel me into your walled city
and leave me there overnight
like the centrepiece of a fountain,
something people piss on
once the streetlights dim
or throw pennies into
when they want the sky
to know they're sorry.

One of these days,
I'll silently explode
and all of the tiny soldiers
I've held inside of me
will open barricades,
burn this place to the ground.
Hear that? It's the soft sizzle,
the creaking panels,
the slow realisation
that I, no matter what you first thought,
am not hollow.

SHEEP EYES

The night of the rejection, I turned
onto the empty road
and tried to keep my eyes open
but anyone who has driven the N59
knows there is no darkness like it –
smothering the headlight
like a fat stomach stopping a punch.
So, imagine my surprise when I saw
not one, but four of them hovering
and soon more – higher, further,
everywhere,
reflecting my lonely beams
like valuable things reflect the sun.
I got out, went down on my hunkers
to join this new choir,
waiting for the next driver
to struggle through small hours
so that I might sit up straight,
hold still my twitching eyelids,
bounce back their blinding light.

BALD EAGLE

It has a bad wing.
Hit on the road, you say,
rehabilitated, hobbling
on a branch
like an early draft of the Pixar lamp.
Still, you can see why
it is the symbol of a country –
that stern stare, the jagged unpredict-
able head-turns
commanding us to stay still,
to try and imagine what it sees.
We're rooted to the spot
in the other-worldly heat,
your skin smooth, my arm
around your waist
bent and feathered.
It's a majestic thing, regardless
of injury
regardless of all the bad things
we might say about it,
regardless of whether either of us
is ready to fly.

CERULEAN

The day you lay on a kitchen floor
slippery with tears and snot,
I was at a seal demonstration
in a Lanzarote park,
watching the well-behaved pups
arf and clap their flippers.
On the other side of the glass,
I watched one glide through blue
so deftly, yet alone.

Back then you felt as though people
are destined never to be happy,
but I had never been happier
posing for the souvenir photo,
the seal pressing whiskered lips
to my cheek.

I did not realise then
that kissing seal was you.
I watched you stand up
on two strong webbed feet,
cross cold callous tiles,
put water in between us.

Seals are built for water
but you remade yourself without it,
so much that I mistook you for a person
when we finally met again,
the skin below your neck
suspiciously smooth.

On New Year's Eve
as we dance along the canal,
I see the water gleam
in the hungry mouth of your eyes.
Tonight, the fireworks watch us
through the glass window.
The room is cerulean,
you are floating in it,
but this time, I am in it with you,
I am holding onto you
for dear life.

THE PIKE

Ross Lake's tiny island
saps a sun on its downward call;
we cannot wait much longer.
Marie's 83 this winter, he tells me,
wants her own son to stay away
to keep the virus outside her walls

because it's already here in the village
thanks to the junior team above in Stronger's,
their rivals conquered,
partying and infesting one another,
the kind of long-awaited for knowledge
of a woman who misses being a mother.

'No crowds on the water today'
he jokes, telling then of great scores
at Oughterard's Mayfly contests, young lads
who'd jump in when a bite took, emerge on all fours
wrestling glossy trophies, glad
only about what a local paper would say.

'Have you fished yourself?' he asks
and I see suddenly the pier in Cork
where I nearly landed a monster.
'Feed the handle. That's it.' My mother's calm talk
as my line pulled as much as it could muster
through an ocean that basked

in resisting my heaving fight.
After the final tug, I watched
old Molloy's rod disappear in the deep,
my heart yanked down with it.
Though she told me she was proud, I didn't sleep,
made a silent vow through the awful night.

Before I can answer, the line whips straight,
pink maggots in their bucket squirm alert
as a silver tail whirls up, reverts
underwater, making the nimble reeds thrash
curt. The pike. Teeth to gnash
through a man's bone if he's careless removing bait.

And as though he senses what I haven't said,
he passes the straining pole over,
I knock evening cold from my palms,
leave no handle-turning yard unfed
as scales of glee lift and dance
the dying light back to me.

AUDITORIUM

They have all gotten the invitation
and most come
one or two, a little late.
I watch them from behind the curtain
select their seats carefully,
weigh each other up.
Some chat in the easy way
women have with one another.
Others sit facing forward,
their belongings clutched tightly
in their laps. One has dyed
her hair, one has lost weight,
one is surprised to see someone she knows.
Most realise at last why they are here,
how it all makes sense now.
But there are outliers – an American girl
whose name I can't remember
wonders if she has come through the right door.
When the house lights dim,
and voices hush one by one,
I walk out onto the stage.
It's nothing they haven't seen before
but I still feel the need to cover myself.
I stand for a few moments,
breathe myself into the ground.

Then, forgiving applause.
I shake each hand as they file out –
catch up enthusiastically with some.
With others, return a curt nod.
When at last the auditorium is empty,
I get up and give a shout to the tiered rows,
just to have my voice break
all that naked silence.

An Otter at Sunrise

Still, I cannot blame him
as he picks through litter
bobbing empty near his fur:
film cartons and paint tubs,
an old guitar and poetry book,
thrown out by harsh water on a whim.

If his dam broke apart now,
scattering down the thin creek,
he thinks the clutter he still seeks
will help him to float
but like me, he's yet to note
that when it's time to swim, he'll know how.

How to Make a Dreamer

Take bones, skin, hair and clothes.
Muscle, either waned
or pulp as ripe fruit. Take pulse,
ticking and blinking by the half-second.
This will be the body,
the footballer's shoulders,
the flutist's fingers.
Then, the voice. Look for this
in the strangest of places;
rub rocks together, struggle
with a blocked tap, crackle twigs
on forest bedding.
Use these to make the sounds –
calls of joy or regret,
the shouts of encouragement.
Select a special type of air –
not the smog from cluttered cities,
but from the alcove created
between two sleeping kayaks –
as the breath.
Now, we have life
created from life,
the life that blushes and twinkles
from all angles.
Next, mould a set of hands
from beach clay.
Watch as they clench and relax,
spread over a blank notepad,
trace the spine on their owner's back.
Give them an instrument; a paintbrush,
pen, chisel, oar,
see how the sculpt the world around them
like sleep sculpts dreams.

Lastly, take a tiny candle-thread
rooted in wax. Let this be love;
whatever is to be wanted
or tried for over this place.
Blow onto them, fan the flame
like you would a Chinese lantern.
Release them from your palm,
watch as they climb the endless sky
and float, float
and rise and rise.

DANCING MONKEY

He follows me everywhere.
In crowds he goes down a treat –
people clap in time with his fervent bounces
and when they don't, he dances
a little harder.

Even when we're in cafés,
trying to share a quiet Americano,
he starts making faces for nearby children
in high-risers, and won't stop
until he turns a cry into a laugh.

His dancing has taken me to faraway places –
an icy subway platform in New York,
lion scouting in Zambia,
the belly of a 100-foot whale.
His waltzing drove away

more than one best friend.
Of course, I would give out about this
if I hadn't just now entered
the curtained room without a mirror
because I heard a clatter.

And through a gap in the door,
his limbs moving
to some invisible ever-changing algorithm,
I see myself, eyes closed,
dancing for my life.